MANUAL 2:
THE FUNERAL PLANNING GUIDE

STEP-BY-STEP ARRANGEMENTS

STEPHANIE OLDS

Printed in the United States of America
First Edition—Second Printing, May 2025

ISBN: 978-1968178093

Ink and Revival Publishing
Virginia, USA

Welcome

Planning a funeral is one of the most difficult tasks a family will ever face. When a loved one passes, emotions are high, and the weight of making important decisions—often in a short amount of time—canfeel overwhelming. I know this firsthand. When my motherpassed away, there were so many details to figure out, but having a plan in place made all the difference. It allowed me to focus on my grief and my family, rather than feeling lost in a sea of choices.

The truth is, funerals come with many decisions—some big, some small, but all important. What kind of service will honor your loved one best? How do you choose a funeral home? What are the costs, and how can you plan within a budget? These are tough questions, but you don't have to face them alone.

This guideis designed to walk you through the funeral planningprocess step by step. Whether you are making arrangements in advance or facing them unexpectedly, my hope is that this resource will provide clarity, comfort, and direction during a difficult time.

Thank you for allowingme to be part of your journey.I hope this guide helps bring peace of mind to you and your family.

WHAT'S INSIDE

- ✓ **Types of Funerals** – Traditional burial, cremation, green burials, and memorial services.

- ✓ **Choosing a Funeral Home** – What to ask, comparing prices, and understanding funeral packages.

- ✓ **Funeral Costs and Budgeting** – Common expenses, prepaid plans, and financial assistance options.

- ✓ **Writing an Obituary** – What to include and sample templates.

- ✓ **Planning the Service** – Venue options, religious or non-religious services, music, and speakers.

- ✓ **Burial or Cremation Decisions** – Cemetery plots, urns, and scattering ashes.

WHY PLANNING A FUNERAL MATTERS

Most people don't realize just how many decisions go into planning a funeral—until they're forced to do it under stress and grief. From choosing between burial or cremation to deciding on service details, obituary wording, and even transportation costs, the process can quickly become overwhelming. But planning ahead, even just knowing what to expect, can make all the difference.

Did you know that **the average funeral with burial in 2023 cost between $8,000 and $10,000,** while a cremation with a service averaged **$6,000 to $7,000**? Without preparation, families often struggle to cover these expenses, sometimes taking on unexpected debt. Even beyond cost, many families are left unsure about what their loved one would have wanted—leading to rushed decisions and added emotional strain.

This guide will walk you through the funeral planning process step by step, helping you make informed choices that fit your family's needs, values, and budget. Whether you're planning for yourself or arranging services for a loved one, taking the time to understand your options now can help ensure a meaningful, affordable, and stress-free farewell when the time comes.

Let's begin—because preparation today means peace of mind tomorrow.

Table of Contents

Section 1

Types of Funerals

Funeral Planning 101

Section 1: Types of Funerals

Funerals can be personalized to fit religious, cultural, and personal beliefs. Common options include:

- **Traditional Burial** – Includes a viewing, service, and burial in a cemetery.
- **Cremation** – The body is cremated, and ashes may be kept, scattered, or buried.
- **Green Burial** – An eco-friendly burial without embalming or a traditional casket.
- **Memorial Service** – A ceremony without the body present, held at a later date.

Understanding Your Options Across Cultures and Religions

Funerals, which are an important way for family and friends to honor a loved one's life and say goodbye, are deeply personal and often shaped by religious beliefs, cultural traditions, and family values. While most people choose traditional burial, cremation, green burial, or memorial services, different cultures and faiths have their own unique practices for honoring the deceased.

Traditional Burial

A traditional burial is one of the most common funeral choices in the United States. It usually includes:

- A **viewing or visitation**, where family and friends gather to see the deceased and offer condolences.
- A **funeral service**, which may take place in a funeral home, church, or other location.
- A **burial in a cemetery**, with a casket placed in the ground.

However, different cultures have specific customs:

- ➢ **Christian Funerals** – Many Christian families hold a **wake or visitation** before the funeral, followed by a church or graveside service. Catholic funerals often include a **Mass of Christian Burial** with prayers for the deceased.

- ➢ **Jewish Funerals** – In Judaism, burial takes place as soon as possible, usually within **24 hours**. Embalming is avoided, and the body is wrapped in a simple **white shroud (tachrichim)** before being placed in a plain wooden coffin. After burial, the family observes a mourning period called **Shiva**, where visitors offer support.

> **?**
>
> **Did you know?**
> The average cost of a traditional burial in the U.S. was **$8,000–$10,000 in 2023**, including the casket, funeral home services, and cemetery plot (*National Funeral Directors Association*).

- ➤ **Muslim Funerals** – Islamic traditions require a swift burial, usually within **24 hours**. The body is washed, wrapped in a simple **white cloth (kafan)**, and buried facing Mecca. Cremation is not permitted in Islam.

- ➤ **Hispanic and Latin American Funerals** – Many Hispanic and Latin American families hold **vigils, prayers, and large family gatherings** before and after the burial. Mourning periods can last several days, and religious customs, such as Catholic **rosary services**, are common.

Cremation

Cremation is becoming increasingly popular, with **more than 59% of Americans choosing cremation over burial as of 2023** (*NFDA*). The body is reduced to ashes through high heat, and families have several options for what to do with the remains:

- **Keep the ashes** in an urn at home.
- **Scatter the ashes** in a meaningful place.
- **Bury the ashes** in a cemetery or memorial garden.

Cremation tends to be more affordable than traditional burial, with an average cost of **$6,000–$7,000** when a service is included.

Cremation is becoming more popular, but it is not accepted by all cultures and religions:

Hindu Funerals – In Hinduism, cremation is a sacred tradition, as it is believed to release the soul from the body. The ashes are often scattered in a sacred river, such as the Ganges in India.

Buddhist Funerals – Many Buddhists choose cremation, following the example of the Buddha himself. Families often keep the ashes in a shrine or temple, while others scatter them in a meaningful place.

Jewish and Muslim Traditions – Both Judaism and Islam traditionally forbid cremation, believing that the body should remain intact for burial. However, some Reform Jewish communities have begun to accept cremation as a personal choice.

Green Burial

Green burials are an eco-friendly option that avoids embalming chemicals, metal caskets, or concrete vaults. Instead, the body is placed in a biodegradable coffin or wrapped in a cloth, allowing for natural decomposition. Some green cemeteries even plant trees instead of traditional headstones.

> **(?)** **Did you know?** The Green Burial Council reports that **interest in green burials has increased by 72% in the past decade**, as more people seek environmentally friendly funeral options.

Green burials are growing in popularity across different cultures, as they align with spiritual beliefs about returning to nature:

➤ **Indigenous and Native American Funerals** – Many Indigenous tribes view burial as a way to return the body to the earth naturally. Some tribes perform traditional ceremonies, such as smudging (burning sacred herbs) or singing to guide the soul's journey.

➤ **Eco-Friendly Christian Funerals** – Some Christian communities now embrace green burials, believing that avoiding embalming and metal caskets is more in line with biblical teachings about caring for creation.

Memorial Service

A memorial service is different from a traditional funeral because the body is not present. Families may hold the service days, weeks, or even months after the person has passed. This allows time for planning and can be more flexible in terms of location and cost. Memorial services can be held at a:

- Church, funeral home, or community center.
- Park, beach, or other outdoor location.
- Family home with a private gathering.

➤ **African American Homegoing Services** – Many Black communities hold "homegoing" services, which celebrate the deceased's journey to the afterlife with joyful music, storytelling, and religious messages.

➤ **Japanese and Chinese Funerals** – In Japan and China, memorial services can take place weeks or months after cremation, as families observe ancestral remembrance rituals such as Obon (Japan) or Qingming (China), where they visit graves and make offerings.

(?) **Did you know?** According to the NFDA, **nearly 40%** of families now choose memorial services over traditional funerals because they allow for more personalization.

Choosing the Right Funeral Option

There is no right or wrong way to plan a funeral—it depends on personal wishes, religious beliefs, and financial circumstances. Each culture and religion has its own way of honoring the deceased, but ultimately, the best choice is one that reflects personal values, traditions, and financial circumstances. Understanding these options ahead of time can help families make the best decision when the time comes. Planning ahead helps ensure that the funeral follows the wishes of the deceased and their family.

Section 2

Funeral Homes

Section 2: Choosing a Funeral Home

When selecting a funeral home, it's important to:

- Compare **prices** (ask for a written price list).
- Ask about **service options** (do they allow customization?).
- Check **reviews** or get recommendations from friends.
- Understand **transportation costs** (some charge extra for long distances).

What You Need to Know – The Basics

Selecting a funeral home is one of the most important decisions in the funeral planning process. Not all funeral homes offer the same services, and prices can vary widely. Knowing what to look for can help families make the best choice based on their needs, budget, and personal preferences.

1. Compare Prices

Funeral costs can be expensive, and they add up quickly. That's why it's important to **compare prices** before making a decision.

By law, **all funeral homes in the U.S. are required to provide a written price list upon request** (*Federal Trade Commission's Funeral Rule*). Families should ask for this list and compare services to find the best option within their budget.

Tip: Some funeral homes offer **"package deals,"** but it's important to check whether all included services are necessary. Families may be able to **save money by choosing only the specific services they need.**

2. Ask About Service Options

Not all funeral homes provide the same services, so families should ask about what is available. Some important questions to consider include:

- ✓ Can the service be personalized? (e.g., music, flowers, photo displays)
- ✓ Does the funeral home offer both **burial and cremation** options?
- ✓ Is there an **onsite chapel** for services?
- ✓ Can they help with **paperwork and legal requirements**, such as death certificates?
- ✓ Do they provide **livestreaming or recording services** for family members who can't attend?

Customization matters. According to the NFDA (2023), more than 50% of families now request nontraditional funeral services, such as outdoor ceremonies, themed celebrations, or home-based memorials. If personalization is important, it's best to ask upfront.

3. Check Reviews and Ask for Recommendations

Not all funeral homes have the same reputation. Some may have excellent customer service, while others may be difficult to work with. To find a trusted funeral home:

- ✓ Read **online reviews** on Google, Yelp, or the funeral home's website.
- ✓ Ask **friends, family, or religious leaders** for recommendations.
- ✓ Check if the funeral home is accredited by professional organizations like the **NFDA (National Funeral Directors Association)**.

Why is this important? A survey by the Consumer Federation of America (2023) found that over 20% of families reported feeling pressured into expensive funeral services they didn't need. Choosing a highly rated, well-reviewed funeral home can help avoid this issue.

4. Understand Transportation Costs

If the funeral home is far from where the service or burial will take place, families may have to pay extra fees for **transporting the body**. Some important details to check:

- ✓ **Local vs. Long-Distance Transfers** – Some funeral homes charge by the mile if the burial site is far away.
- ✓ **Out-of-State Funerals** – If the deceased needs to be transported to another state or country, special permits and airline costs may apply.
- ✓ **Hearse and Family Vehicles** – Many funeral homes charge extra for transporting family members in limousines or service cars.

💡 **Tip:** Ask for a detailed breakdown of **all transportation fees** before signing any contracts.

Final Thoughts

Choosing a funeral home is a major decision, and it's okay to take time to compare options. Families should ask questions, get written price lists, and read reviews to find a funeral home that meets their needs. By planning ahead, families can reduce financial stress, avoid unnecessary costs, and ensure a meaningful farewell for their loved one.

Additional Details on Funeral Home Services & Hidden Costs

When choosing a funeral home, it's important to understand **exactly what services are included** and **what additional costs might come up**. Some expenses are standard, while others may be optional or hidden in package pricing. Below is a breakdown of common services and potential extra costs families should be aware of.

1. *Common Funeral Home Services*

Most funeral homes offer a range of services to assist with planning and handling arrangements. Some of the most common include:

- ✓ **Body Preparation** – Includes embalming, dressing, hairstyling, and makeup for viewings.
- ✓ **Funeral Service Coordination** – Scheduling the viewing, funeral, and burial with the family and venue.
- ✓ **Cremation Services** – Some funeral homes have on-site crematories, while others outsource the service to third parties.
- ✓ **Paperwork Assistance** – Handling death certificates, permits, and insurance claims on behalf of the family.
- ✓ **Casket/Urn Sales** – Many funeral homes sell caskets, urns, and burial vaults. However, families are not required to buy from the funeral home and can purchase from other providers.
- ✓ **Memorial Printing & Programs** – Many offer custom obituaries, memorial cards, and guest books for the service.

💡 **Tip:** Some funeral homes offer "all-inclusive" packages, but families should always ask for a detailed itemized price list before agreeing to a package.

2. *Hidden or Unexpected Costs*

Some funeral homes **do not clearly disclose all costs upfront**, leading families to **pay for services they may not have planned for**. Here are some common hidden costs to watch out for:

- ☐ **Embalming Fees ($600–$1,000)** – Embalming is only required by law in certain cases, such as long-distance transport of the body. However, some funeral homes may automatically include it unless the family specifically requests direct burial or cremation.
- ☐ **Casket Markups ($1,200–$5,000)** – Many funeral homes sell caskets at a premium, but families are legally allowed to buy one from an outside provider (like Costco or online retailers) and cannot be charged extra for using a third-party casket (*FTC Funeral Rule*).
- ☐ **Funeral Home "Facility Fees" ($400–$1,000)** – Some funeral homes charge extra just for using their chapel or reception area for a service.
- ☐ **Transportation & Hearse Fees ($300–$500)** – Some funeral homes charge extra fees per mile for transporting the body beyond a certain distance.

- ☐ **Weekend or Holiday Service Fees ($200–$500)** – Funerals held on weekends or holidays may cost extra due to staffing costs.
- ☐ **Obituary Placement Fees ($200–$600)** – Some newspapers charge per word or per line, which can add up quickly if publishing an obituary in multiple places.
- ☐ **Extra Copies of Death Certificates ($10–$25 each)** – Many financial institutions and insurance companies require original copies of the death certificate. Families should ask the funeral home how many they need.

💡 **Tip:** If a funeral home insists on certain services that seem unnecessary, families should **ask if they are legally required** or simply recommended.

3. *How to Avoid Overpaying for Funeral Services*

To prevent overspending, families should:

- ☐ **Request a full price list upfront** – Funeral homes are legally required to provide a General Price List (GPL) when asked.
- ☐ **Compare prices at multiple funeral homes** – Costs can vary by thousands of dollars between different providers.
- ☐ **Ask for a breakdown of package deals** – Some packages include unnecessary services that can be removed.
- ☐ **Consider alternative options** – Direct cremation or green burial can significantly reduce costs.
- ☐ **Check for veteran, government, or religious benefits** – Some organizations provide financial assistance or free burial plots for qualifying individuals.

Final Thoughts

Funeral homes provide an essential service, but it's important to be aware of hidden costs and ask the right questions before making decisions. Families should take the time to compare prices, understand their options, and only pay for the services that truly matter to them.

Section 3

Costs and Budgeting

Section 3: Funeral Costs, Budgeting, and How to Save Money

Funerals can be expensive, and many families are unprepared for the costs. These prices can place a significant financial burden on families, especially when arrangements need to be made quickly. However, understanding funeral expenses, knowing your rights, and exploring cost-saving options can help families make informed decisions.

1. Common Funeral Costs

Funeral costs vary based on location, service choices, and personal preferences. Below are the most common expenses:

Major Expenses

- **Casket or Urn** – A standard casket costs $2,500 to $5,000, while high-end models can exceed $10,000. Cremation urns typically cost between $50 and $500.
- **Funeral Home Services** – Embalming ($600–$1,000), body preparation, viewing ($400–$1,000), and transportation ($300–$500) are often included.
- **Cemetery Plot & Headstone** – A public cemetery burial plot can cost $1,000 to $4,000, while private cemeteries may charge more. Headstones range from $1,000 to $3,000.
- **Flowers, Programs, & Memorial Items** – Custom funeral programs, flowers, and keepsakes can cost between $200 and $1,500.

Hidden or Unexpected Costs

- **Grave Opening & Closing Fees** – Cemeteries often charge $500–$1,500 for digging and covering the grave.
- **Hearse & Family Vehicle Rental** – Funeral homes charge $300–$500 for transportation.
- **Weekend or Holiday Fees** – Some funeral homes add $200–$500 for services on non-business days.
- **Obituary Placement Fees** – Many newspapers charge $200–$600, depending on length and publication.
- **Extra Death Certificates** – Many financial institutions require original copies, which cost $10–$25 each.

Tip: Funeral homes must provide a General Price List (GPL) upon request (Federal Trade Commission Funeral Rule). Families should ask for this list and remove unnecessary services to save money.

2. Ways to Reduce Funeral Costs

Funeral expenses can quickly add up, but there are several ways to lower costs while still honoring a loved one:

- ✓ **Prepaid Funeral Plans** – Some people choose to prepay for funeral expenses to lock in prices. However, some prepaid plans have restrictions or hidden fees, so families should review the details carefully.
- ✓ **Direct Cremation ($1,000–$3,000)** – This is one of the most affordable options, eliminating embalming and viewing costs. **Cremation rates in the U.S. reached nearly 60% in 2023** (*NFDA*).
- ✓ **Simple Burial ($2,500–$5,000)** – A burial without embalming, an expensive casket, or a formal service can save thousands.
- ✓ **Buying a Casket or Urn Elsewhere** – Funeral homes *mark up casket prices by 200–400%*, but families can purchase caskets or urns from **Costco, Walmart, or online retailers** for significantly lower prices.
- ✓ **Holding a Service at Home or in a Community Space** – Hosting a memorial at *home, a park, or a religious center* instead of a funeral home can reduce costs.

💡 **Tip:** Funeral homes may push **"package deals,"** but families are **not required** to purchase all services. Always ask for an **itemized breakdown** to remove unnecessary charges.

3. Understanding Funeral Home Policies & Negotiating Costs

Many people don't realize that **funeral prices are negotiable** and that families have legal rights when selecting services.

Know Your Rights

Under the **FTC Funeral Rule**, funeral homes **must:**

- ✓ Provide an **itemized price list** (so families can compare costs).
- ✓ Allow families to **decline services** they don't need.
- ✓ Accept caskets and urns **purchased from third-party retailers** without extra fees.
- ✓ Not require **embalming** unless state law mandates it for transportation.

💡 **Tip:** If a funeral home refuses to provide pricing details or pressures families into costly services, they can be reported to the FTC or local consumer protection agency.

How to Negotiate & Lower Costs

- ☐ **Get multiple quotes** – Prices can vary **by thousands of dollars** between different funeral homes.

- ☐ **Ask about direct burial or cremation options** – These are often the most affordable choices.
- ☐ **Remove unnecessary add-ons** – Fancy caskets, luxury vehicles, and premium flower arrangements are ***optional***.
- ☐ **Use life insurance or assistance programs** – Many policies cover funeral expenses if a claim is filed promptly.

♀ **Tip:** Some funeral homes offer payment plans for families who need financial flexibility.

4. Financial Assistance for Funeral Costs

For families struggling to cover funeral expenses, there are **government and nonprofit programs** that can help:

- ✓ **Veterans' Benefits** – The **Department of Veterans Affairs (VA)** provides eligible veterans:
  - Free burial in a national cemetery, including a headstone and burial flag.
  - A funeral reimbursement of up to $2,000 for service-related deaths.
  - A burial allowance ($300–$893) for non-service-related deaths.
  - How to Apply: Visit www.va.gov or call 1-800-827-1000.

- ✓ **Social Security Death Benefit** – The Social Security Administration provides a one-time payment of $255 to a surviving spouse or child.
  - How to Apply: Call 1-800-772-1213 or visit www.ssa.gov.

- ✓ **State & Local Assistance** – Medicaid & State Burial Assistance – Some states offer funeral assistance for low-income families, often covering basic cremation or burial.
  - Check with local Human Services or Medicaid offices for state-specific programs.
  - County Indigent Burial Programs – Many counties provide free or low-cost burial or cremation for unclaimed or indigent individuals.
  - Contact local government offices or public health departments for eligibility.
  - Nonprofit & Religious Assistance
  - The Final Farewell Program – Helps low-income families cover burial costs for children. (www.finalfarewell.org)
  - Jewish Free Burial Association & Islamic Burial Funds – Many religious organizations provide burial aid for community members in need.

- Contact local churches, mosques, or synagogues for available assistance.
- ✓ **Crowdfunding & Community Support** – Many families use GoFundMe or local charities to raise money for funeral costs. Some religious organizations also provide funeral aid.

💡 **Tip:** If financial assistance isn't enough, some families opt for "body donation programs," which cover cremation costs in exchange for donating the body to medical research.

Final Thoughts

Funeral costs can be overwhelming, but with *careful planning, price comparisons, and financial assistance,* families can create a meaningful service without unnecessary financial stress.

Low-Cost Memorial Alternatives

For families facing financial hardship, there are various assistance programs and low-cost alternatives to traditional funerals. Exploring these options can help reduce expenses while still honoring a loved one in a meaningful way.

1. Low-Cost Funeral & Memorial Alternatives

If traditional funerals are too expensive, families can consider **affordable alternatives** that still provide a meaningful way to say goodbye.

Low-Cost Funeral Options

- **Direct Cremation ($1,000–$3,000)** – This is the cheapest funeral option, eliminating embalming and viewing costs. Many families scatter ashes in a meaningful location instead of purchasing a burial plot.
- **Home Funerals ($500–$2,000)** – Some states allow family-led funerals at home, avoiding funeral home fees. Families can wash, dress, and hold a private service before burial or cremation.
- **Green Burials ($2,500–$5,000)** – Natural burials skip embalming and use biodegradable caskets, reducing costs while being environmentally friendly.
  - Visit www.greenburialcouncil.org for certified locations.

Affordable Memorial Alternatives

- **Online Memorials (Free–$100)** – Websites like GatheringUs, Ever Loved, or Facebook Memorial Pages allow families to create virtual tributes with photos, videos, and guest messages.
- **DIY Memorial Service (Low-Cost)** – Instead of renting a funeral home, families can hold a memorial gathering at home, a park, or a religious center with personal tributes, music, and photos.
- **Tree Planting Memorial ($50–$300)** – Organizations like The Arbor Day Foundation plant a tree in honor of a loved one, providing a lasting tribute.
- **Cremation Jewelry or Memorial Art ($100–$500)** – Ashes can be placed into necklaces, glass art, or tattoos as a permanent keepsake.

Tip: Some families skip expensive headstones and opt for engraved memorial benches or plaques in community spaces for a lasting tribute.

Final Thoughts

No family should have to go into debt to honor a loved one. By exploring assistance programs, affordable funeral options, and creative memorial ideas, families can find a meaningful and budget-friendly way to say goodbye.

Section 4

Writing an Obituary

Section 4: Writing an Obituary

An obituary is a short notice about a person's life and passing. It usually includes:

- Full name and age
- Date and place of birth and death
- Surviving family members
- Details of the funeral or memorial service
- A brief summary of their life and achievements

Custom Obituary Templates & Writing Tips for Different Cultures and Religions

Obituaries can be written in different styles depending on personal, cultural, and religious traditions. Below are custom templates and tips to help families create a meaningful tribute.

1. Basic Obituary Template (Traditional Format)

This template follows a **classic newspaper obituary style**:

[Full Name], [Age], of [City, State], passed away on [Date] at [Location, if desired]. [He/She/They] was born on [Birthdate] in [Birthplace] to [Parents' Names].

[First Name] was a [mention profession, role, or key life detail]. [He/She/They] enjoyed [list hobbies, passions, or interests] and was known for [mention a unique trait or achievement].

[First Name] is survived by [list close family members, such as spouse, children, siblings, grandchildren]. [He/She/They] was preceded in death by [mention predeceased loved ones].

A [funeral/memorial service] will be held on **[Date, Time] at [Location]**. In lieu of flowers, donations can be made to **[Charity or Organization]** in [First Name]'s honor.

Example:

> **John Robert Williams, 67, of Chicago, Illinois, passed away on April 5, 2024, surrounded by his family. He was born on February 12, 1957, in Detroit, Michigan, to Charles and Martha Williams.**
>
> John was a devoted husband, father, and grandfather. He worked as a firefighter for 30 years and loved fishing, playing guitar, and spending time with his grandchildren. He will always be remembered for his kindness and dedication to helping others.
>
> John is survived by his wife, Linda, his two children, Sarah (Mark) and David (Jennifer), and his four grandchildren. He was preceded in death by his parents and his brother, James.
>
> A memorial service will be held on **April 10, 2024, at 2:00 PM at St. Mark's Church in Chicago**. In lieu of flowers, donations may be made to the **Chicago Firefighters Foundation** in his honor.

2. Short & Simple Obituary Template

This is a **brief version** for newspapers with word limits or families who prefer a simple announcement.

[Full Name], [Age], of [City, State], passed away on [Date]. [He/She/They] was born on [Birthdate] in [Birthplace].

[First Name] is survived by [list family members]. A [funeral/memorial service] will be held on **[Date, Time] at [Location]**.

💡 **Tip:** Many newspapers charge per word for obituaries. Keeping it short can reduce costs while still sharing important details.

3. Obituary Templates for Different Cultures and Religions

Many cultures and faiths have unique obituary styles. Below are tailored templates to reflect these traditions.

Christian Obituary

Christian obituaries often mention faith, church involvement, and beliefs about the afterlife.

"With faith in God, we announce the passing of [Full Name], who was called home on [Date] at the age of [Age]. Born in [Birthplace] on [Birthdate], [First Name] dedicated [his/her/their] life to family, faith, and serving others."

A devoted member of [Church Name], [First Name] enjoyed [hobbies, community service, or faith-related roles]. [He/She/They] is now at peace in the presence of the Lord.

A celebration of life will be held at [Church Name] on [Date, Time]. In lieu of flowers, donations may be made to [Church/Religious Charity].

Jewish Obituary

Jewish obituaries are often simple and respectful, following the belief in honoring the deceased with dignity.

"With deep sorrow, we announce the passing of [Full Name] on [Date] at the age of [Age]. Born on [Birthdate], [First Name] was a beloved [relation, e.g., father, sister, grandparent] and cherished member of [Synagogue/Community]."

The funeral will be held on [Date] at [Location]. Shiva will be observed at [Family Residence] from [Dates]. Donations in [First Name]'s memory may be made to [Jewish Charity or Organization]. May [his/her/their] memory be a blessing.

💡 **Tip:** Jewish funerals often take place quickly after death, so obituary notices may be brief and focus on funeral details and Shiva information.

Islamic Obituary
Islamic obituaries focus on prayer and submission to God's will, as cremation is generally not practiced in Islam.

"Inna lillahi wa inna ilayhi raji'un (To God we belong and to Him we return). It is with great sadness that we announce the passing of [Full Name] on [Date]. [First Name] was a loving [relation] and a faithful servant of Allah."

A Janazah (funeral) prayer will be held at [Mosque or Funeral Location] on [Date, Time], followed by burial at [Cemetery Name]. We ask for your duas (prayers) and support during this time.

💡 **Tip:** Islamic traditions emphasize simplicity and humility. Families often request charitable donations (Sadaqah) in the deceased's honor.

Buddhist Obituary
Buddhist obituaries highlight peace, karma, and reincarnation.

"We honor the peaceful passing of [Full Name] on [Date] at the age of [Age]. A kind and compassionate soul, [First Name] lived a life of wisdom and generosity, bringing light to all who knew [him/her/them]."

A memorial ceremony will be held at [Temple Name] on [Date, Time]. May [his/her/their] journey continue in peace and enlightenment. In lieu of flowers, offerings may be made to [Buddhist Organization or Temple].

---

4. Modern & Personalized Obituary Ideas
For families who want a nontraditional or more personalized obituary, here are some ideas:

➢ **Storytelling Approach** – Instead of a formal style, write the obituary as a short story about the person's life, humor, or favorite memories.

➢ **Social Media Tributes** – Many families create video memorials, digital guestbooks, or Facebook pages to share photos and stories.

➢ **Poetic or Quote-Based** – Some obituaries begin with a favorite poem, quote, or lyrics that reflect the deceased's personality.

➢ **List Format** – A unique approach is listing the person's favorite things, such as movies, books, sayings, or achievements.

Example of a Fun & Personal Obituary:

> *"The world became a little less bright on March 15, 2024, when John Smith, 62, of Nashville, TN, traded in his earthly boots for a front-row seat at the biggest rock concert in the sky. Born on July 10, 1961, John spent his life telling dad jokes, playing guitar, and cheering for the Titans (even when they lost). He leaves behind his wife of 35 years, two kids, and a dog that secretly loved him more than anyone else."*

Final Thoughts

An obituary is more than just an announcement—it is a chance to celebrate a life well lived. Whether following religious traditions or writing a unique, personalized tribute, the key is to reflect the true spirit of the person being remembered.

Section 5

Planning the Service

Section 5: Planning the Service

Funeral services can be simple or elaborate, depending on personal and cultural preferences. Key elements to consider:

- **Location** – Funeral home, church, park, or even a home gathering.
- **Speakers** – Family members, friends, religious leaders.
- **Music and Readings** – Hymns, favorite songs, poetry, or scripture.
- **Display of Memories** – Photos, videos, or personal items.

Planning a Funeral Service: A Step-by-Step Guide

A funeral service is an important way for family and friends to honor and remember a loved one. Some funerals are simple and private, while others are larger and more elaborate, depending on family traditions, religious beliefs, and personal wishes.

Did you know? In a 2023 survey by the National Funeral Directors Association (NFDA), 60% of families said they preferred a personalized funeral service over a traditional one.

Planning ahead can help create a meaningful and comforting service for those who are grieving.

1. Choosing the Location

The funeral service can be held in different places, depending on cultural traditions, religious practices, and personal preferences.

Common Funeral Locations:

- **Funeral Home** – Provides professional service and seating for guests.
- **Church or Religious Center** – Suitable for families who want a faith-based service.
- **Park or Outdoor Setting** – A natural and peaceful option for informal gatherings.
- **Family Home** – More intimate and private, allowing for a personal touch.

Tip: Some families also choose virtual services or livestreaming so loved ones from far away can attend.

2. Selecting Speakers

The people who speak at the funeral service help share memories and celebrate the life of the deceased.

Who Can Speak at a Funeral?

- ✓ **Religious Leaders** – If the person was religious, a minister, priest, rabbi, or imam may lead prayers or deliver a eulogy.
- ✓ **Family Members** – Children, spouses, or siblings often share personal stories and memories.
- ✓ **Close Friends** – A best friend or longtime companion may give a heartfelt speech.
- ✓ **Coworkers or Community Members** – If the deceased was active in a profession or community, a representative may speak.

💡 **Tip:** Not everyone is comfortable speaking in public. Families can pre-record messages or have someone read on behalf of others.

3. Choosing Music and Readings

Music and readings can make a funeral **more personal and meaningful**. They reflect the deceased's personality, faith, and the emotions of loved ones.

Music Options

- ✓ **Religious Hymns** – Common in Christian, Jewish, and other faith-based funerals (e.g., "Amazing Grace" or "Ave Maria").
- ✓ **Favorite Songs** – Some families choose meaningful pop, rock, or country songs (e.g., "Somewhere Over the Rainbow").
- ✓ **Instrumental or Live Music** – Soft piano, violin, or acoustic guitar performances can create a peaceful atmosphere.

Readings & Poems

- ✓ **Scripture Passages** – Many religious services include Bible verses, Quranic recitations, or Buddhist sutras.
- ✓ **Poetry & Quotes** – Poems like "Do Not Stand at My Grave and Weep" are commonly read.
- ✓ **Personal Letters or Messages** – Some families write farewell letters to the deceased and read them aloud.

💡 **Tip:** Families should consider recording the service or creating a playlist of the music and readings for those who couldn't attend.

4. Displaying Memories

A funeral service is a time to remember and celebrate a person's life. Displaying personal memories can help guests reflect on happy moments shared with the deceased.

Ways to Display Memories:

- ✓ **Photo Collages or Slideshows** – Show pictures of different stages of life.
- ✓ **Memory Tables** – Set up a table with meaningful items (favorite books,

sports jerseys, artwork).
- ✓ **Video Tribute** – A short video with pictures, clips, and favorite music can be played during the service.
- ✓ **Memory Cards or Guest Books** – Guests can write messages or memories to be kept by the family.

💡 **Tip:** Some families create digital memory books or plant a tree in honor of the deceased as a lasting tribute.

Final Thoughts

Planning a funeral service takes time and thought, but personalizing it with music, readings, and memories makes it more meaningful for everyone attending. Whether small and simple or large and elaborate, the most important thing is that the service honors the life and legacy of the loved one.

Section 6

Burial or Cremation

Section 6: Burial or Cremation Decisions

For burials, families need to choose:

- A **cemetery** (public or private).
- A **grave marker** (headstone or plaque).

For cremation, options include:

- Keeping ashes in an **urn** at home.
- Scattering ashes in a meaningful location.
- Placing ashes in a **columbarium** (a memorial space for urns).

Burial or Cremation Decisions: Understanding Your Options

One of the most important decisions families face when planning a funeral is choosing between burial or cremation. This choice is often based on personal beliefs, religious traditions, and financial considerations. In 2023, nearly 60% of Americans chose cremation over burial, a number that has been increasing due to cost and environmental concerns (*National Funeral Directors Association*).

Understanding the different options for both burial and cremation can help families make the best decision for their loved one.

1. Burial Options
Burial is a traditional and widely accepted funeral choice. It typically involves placing the body in a casket and interring it in a cemetery.

Choosing a Cemetery
Families can select from different types of cemeteries:
- ➢ **Public Cemeteries** – Open to the general public; costs vary by location.
- ➢ **Private Cemeteries** – Often more expensive but may offer additional benefits like private family plots.
- ➢ **Veterans Cemeteries** – Eligible U.S. military veterans can receive free burial in a national cemetery, including a headstone and grave marker (*U.S. Department of Veterans Affairs*).

Cost Considerations: A burial plot in a public cemetery costs between $1,000 and $4,000, while private cemetery plots may exceed $10,000, depending on the location.

Selecting a Grave Marker

A grave marker is placed on the burial site to honor the deceased. Options include:

- **Headstones (Upright Monuments)** – Traditional, standing stones with engraving.
- **Flat Markers (Plaques)** – Simple, ground-level markers, often made of granite or bronze.
- **Mausoleums** – Above-ground burial structures for individuals or families.

Tip: Some cemeteries have restrictions on headstone sizes, materials, or styles—families should check the rules before purchasing a marker.

---

2. Cremation Options

Cremation has become more popular in recent years because it is often more affordable and flexible than burial. The average cremation service in 2023 costs between $1,000 and $3,000, while traditional burials often cost $8,000 or more (*NFDA*).

What Happens After Cremation?

Families have several options for their loved one's ashes:

- ✓ **Keeping the Urn at Home** – Some families choose to keep their loved one's remains in a decorative urn.
- ✓ **Scattering Ashes** – Common locations include beaches, mountains, gardens, or family properties (check local laws before scattering in public places).
- ✓ **Columbarium Placement** – A columbarium is a memorial structure with niches designed to hold urns in a cemetery or church.
- ✓ **Burial of Ashes** – Some families prefer to bury the urn in a cemetery plot with a small grave marker.
- ✓ **Unique Memorials** – Some companies offer options like turning ashes into diamonds, glass art, or even planting them with a tree.

Tip: If scattering ashes in a public location, families should check state lawsâ€"some areas require permits.

---

3. Factors to Consider When Choosing Between Burial and Cremation

When deciding between burial or cremation, families may want to consider the following:

- ➤ **Religious & Cultural Beliefs** – Some faiths, like Islam and Orthodox Judaism, require burial, while Hinduism and Buddhism traditionally favor cremation.

➤ **Environmental Impact** – Green burials and aquamation (water-based cremation) are eco-friendly alternatives gaining popularity.
➤ **Family Preferences** – Some families find comfort in having a physical gravesite, while others prefer the flexibility of cremation.
➤ **Budget** – Cremation is usually more affordable, while burials often involve additional costs like caskets, cemetery fees, and headstones.

Final Thoughts

Both burial and cremation offer meaningful ways to honor a loved one. The right choice depends on personal wishes, cultural traditions, and financial considerations. By understanding all available options, families can make a decision that brings peace and comfort.

Section 7

Workbooks and Checklists

Obituary Writing Worksheet

This step-by-step worksheet is designed to help families gather information and write a meaningful obituary for their loved one. It includes prompts and space to fill in details, making the process easier during a difficult time.

Step 1: Basic Information

Fill in the key details about your loved one.
- **Full Name:** _____
- **Age at Passing:** _____
- **Date of Birth:** _____
- **Place of Birth:** _____
- **Date of Passing:** _____
- **Place of Passing:** _____

Step 2: Family Information

List immediate family members (both surviving and predeceased).
- **Parents:** _____
- **Spouse/Partner:** _____
- **Children (and spouses, if applicable):** _____
- **Siblings:** _____
- **Grandchildren & Great-Grandchildren (optional):**_____
- **Other Important Family Members or Close Friends:** _____

💡 **Tip:** It's common to say "survived by" for living relatives and "preceded in death by" for those who passed earlier.

Step 3: Life Story & Achievements

This section highlights the person's career, hobbies, values, and contributions.
- **Career & Work:** _____
- **Hobbies & Interests:**_____
- **Military Service (if applicable):**_____
- **Community Involvement & Volunteer Work:** _____
- **Personal Traits (e.g., kind, humorous, hardworking):**_____

💡 **Tip:** You can include fun or memorable details about their life, such as their love for fishing, baking, or storytelling.

Step 4: Funeral or Memorial Service Details

Provide information about the service, if applicable.
- **Type of Service (Funeral, Memorial, Celebration of Life, etc.):** _____
- **Date & Time of Service:** _____
- **Location of Service (Funeral Home, Church, Park, etc.):** _____
- **Burial or Cremation Details (if applicable):** _____
- **Who Will Officiate the Service?** _____
- **Special Requests (e.g., "In lieu of flowers, please donate to [charity]"):** _____

Step 5: Drafting the Obituary

Now, use the details above to write a first draft of the obituary.

Obituary Template for Guidance:

"It is with deep sadness that we announce the passing of [Full Name], [Age], of [City, State], on [Date]. Born on [Birthdate] in [Birthplace], [First Name] was a devoted [career or role, such as 'father, teacher, or friend'] who was known for [mention personal qualities or passions]."

"[First Name] is survived by [list family members] and was preceded in death by [mention any deceased relatives]. [He/She/They] enjoyed [list hobbies, work, or community involvement] and will be deeply missed by all who knew them."

"A [funeral/memorial service] will be held at [Location] on [Date, Time]. In lieu of flowers, donations may be made to [Charity or Organization] in [First Name]'s honor."

Step 6: Reviewing & Finalizing

- ✓ **Keep it Clear & Respectful** – The obituary should be easy to read and focus on celebrating the person's life.
- ✓ **Check Word Limits for Newspapers** – Some newspapers charge per word ($200–$600 average cost), so be mindful of length.
- ✓ **Ask Family for Input** – Have at least one other person read the obituary before submitting it.
- ✓ **Decide Where to Publish** – Obituaries can be shared in newspapers, online memorial sites, social media, or community newsletters.

Final Thoughts

Writing an obituary is a way to honor and remember a loved one's life. This worksheet provides a structured approach to make the process easier during an emotional time.

Funeral Service Planning Checklist

This checklist will help families organize and plan a meaningful funeral service. Every funeral is unique, and this guide provides key steps to consider when honoring a loved one.

1. Choose the Location

Select where the service will take place:

- _____

Tip: Consider accessibility for elderly guests and whether the location allows for personal touches.

2. Select Speakers

Decide who will speak or lead the service:

- _____
- _____
- _____

Tip: Not everyone is comfortable speaking in public. Allow guests to write messages that can be read by someone else.

3. Choose Music and Readings

Pick songs, hymns, or readings to be included:

- _____
- _____
- _____

Tip: A recorded playlist of meaningful songs can be shared with guests who couldn't attend.

4. Plan Memory Displays

Decide how to honor the loved one's life visually:

- _____
- _____
- _____

💡 **Tip:** Some families create digital memory books or plant a tree in honor of the deceased as a lasting tribute.

---

5. Organize Service Details

Make sure key logistics are in place:

- _____
- _____
- _____

💡 **Tip:** If hosting a reception afterward, consider providing food and drinks or asking guests to bring a dish.

---

6. Special Requests & Final Touches

Consider any additional elements to personalize the service:

- _____
- _____
- _____

💡 **Tip:** Families can record the service or create a keepsake video to share with future generations.

Final Thoughts

This checklist helps families organize a service that reflects their loved one's values and legacy. Whether traditional or unique, the most important thing is that the service brings comfort and honors the life of the deceased.

Burial vs. Cremation: Decision-Making Checklist

This checklist will help families compare burial and cremation options to make the best choice based on personal, cultural, and financial considerations.

1. Burial Considerations

Cemetery Selection
- _____
- _____
- _____

Grave Marker Options
- _____
- _____
- _____

Burial Cost Considerations
- _____
- _____
- _____

Tip: Some cemeteries have strict rules on headstone sizes, decorations, or maintenance fees—ask before purchasing.

2. Cremation Considerations

Post-Cremation Options
- _____
- _____
- _____

Cremation Cost Considerations
- _____
- _____
- _____

Tip: Many funeral homes offer prepaid cremation plans to lock in lower rates.

3. Important Factors to Consider

Religious & Cultural Beliefs

- _____
- _____
- _____

Environmental Impact

- _____
- _____
- _____

Family Preferences

- _____
- _____
- _____

Budget Comparison

- _____
- _____
- _____

💡 **Tip:** Families should discuss wishes in advance and document decisions in a will or pre-planning guide.

Final Thoughts

This checklist helps families weigh the costs, traditions, and practical aspects of burial and cremation. The right choice is one that aligns with personal values, financial situation, and family preferences.

Funeral Planning Checklist

☐ I have decided on the type of funeral (burial, cremation, green burial, memorial service).
☐ I have chosen a funeral home and reviewed their pricing.
☐ I have considered prepaid funeral options or set aside funds.
☐ I have written down my funeral service preferences (music, speakers, readings).
☐ I have selected a burial location or cremation plan.
☐ I have prepared an obituary or notes for my family to use.
☐ I have designated someone to handle funeral arrangements.

This checklist makes it easier for families to stay organized and ensure they don't overlook important steps.

www.ingramcontent.com/pod-product-compliance
Lightning Source LLC
Chambersburg PA
CBHW081341090426

42737CB00017B/3241